Awaken Your Divine Feminine

A collection of poems compiled by

Annie Gibbins

Copyright © 2023 by **Annie Gibbins**
All rights reserved. No part of this publication may be reproduced, distributed or transmitted in any form or by any means, without prior written permission.

**Annie Gibbins / Women's Biz Publishing
New South Wales, Australia
www.womensbizpublishing.com**

All rights reserved. No part of this book may be used or reproduced by any means, graphic, electronic, or mechanical, including photocopying, recording, taping or by any information storage retrieval system without the written permission of the copyright owner except in the case of brief quotations embodied in critical articles and reviews. Because of the dynamic nature of the Internet, any web addresses or links contained in this book may have changed since publication and may no longer be valid. The views expressed in this work are solely those of the author and do not necessarily reflect the views of the publisher and the publisher hereby disclaims any responsibility for them.

Book Layout © 2023 womensbizpublishing.com
**Awaken Your Divine Feminine /
Annie Gibbins** -- 1st ed.
Paperback ISBN 978-1-922969-11-8

womensbizglobal.com

CONTENTS

UNLEASHING THE DIVINE 5
SHE IS THE FLOWER 7
LOVE LETTER TO SELF 9
THE SACRED VESSEL OF THE DIVINE FEMININE 12
RUMINATION ON THE GLASS CEILING 17
WHEN THE HARP MET THE WOODWIND 20
C.H 23
PERSONAL POWER 24
BRAVE 27
SOUL AND SPIRIT 29
MY BUTTERFLY 31
RISING ABOVE 32
THE MIST ENVELOPES 34
SHE WILL RISE 36
ENCOURAGEMENT ENDURES 38
WE TEACH THEM 40
I AM 42
SUNRISE...44
SHE'S THE AIR I BREATHE 45
WHEN THAT WISP OF WIND 46
HAPPINESS 48
WANT 50
LIKE SUNSHINE 51
IF I CAN SAY THAT I'M FALLING IN LOVE WITH YOU 52
AWAKENING THE GODDESS WITHIN 54
LET ME BE FREE 56
HEARTBEAT 57

FLYING PAST HEAVEN	59
A WOMAN'S WORTH	61
JUST ONE MORE MOMENT	63
FROM THE SEED OF CONCEPTION	65
ALONE BUT NOT LONELY	66
SHE IS SYDNEY	69
THE WILD WOMAN BELIEVES	71
SHE IS NEW ZEALAND	73
THE CAULDRON OF LIFE BECKONED	75
EXPERT ON TRUE LOVE	77
FROM THE SEED OF LIFE	79
SHE IS THE SPIRIT OF ALOHA	81
BLUSH	82
SHE IS DUBAI	85
THE SOUNDS OF EXPRESSION	87
THE BEAUTY BENEATH	89
WHO WILL I CALL	91
THE LOVE POEM	93
DAD	95
LAYING NIGHTLY UPON HER PILLOW	97
HIS STORY	101
PASSION, OR MERELY SUMMER?	103
LIFE PLAYS A TUNE	104
MAKE YOUR MARK	106
GUIDING LIGHT	109
SILENCE OF HER SMILE	112
I AM A DREAM CHASER	114
SHE IS LOVE	116
WELCOME TO ME	118
FEIRCE AND FEMININE	121

ANNIE GIBBINS

In the depths of our beings, sits a wild woman. She is both soft and powerful. She is both forgiving and fierce. She is the symbol of a warrior and a majestic siren. When we look for answers in life, answers that will never present neatly, our divine feminine is unleashed. Together, we are powerful, gentle, soft and relentless, in our pursuit for utter freedom.

Unleashing the Divine

In the depths of the earth and the heights of the sky,
In the oceans that ebb and the mountains that rise,
There is a force that flows through it all,
A power so great, yet humble and small.

She is the divine feminine, a force so strong,
A creator, a nurturer, a healer for so long,
She births life and tends to its growth,
She loves and protects and nurtures our souls.

Her energy is soft and gentle like the breeze,
Yet it can move mountains and uproot trees,

AWAKEN THE DIVINE FEMININE

She is the embodiment of love and grace,
And with every step, she illuminates our space.

Her essence is the light that guides us through the dark,
Her compassion is the fire that ignites our spark,
Her wisdom is the water that quenches our thirst,
And her power is the earth that grounds us first.

She is the goddess, the mother, the divine,
The source of all creation, the light that shines,
She is within us and all around,
In the air we breathe, in the ground we pound.

So let us honour her and embrace her grace,
Let us welcome her love and her warm embrace,
For she is the divine feminine, the eternal flame,
And in her arms, we find our home, our sanctuary, our name.

SHE IS THE FLOWER

JACQUELINE CHERIE WRIGHT

There had been a terrible storm overnight. A big strong tree had fallen across the road. Gutters had also flooded with overflowing water, broken branches, and masses of leaves.

As the storm eased, in the early hours of the morning I drove to the gym. I had been going through a challenging time mentally, emotionally, and physically, so I had committed to strengthening my mind and body by working out no matter rain, hail, or shine. As I arrived, I swung open my car door to scurry out in the rain and wind. I stepped out and caught sight of this beautiful elegant, wild iris weathering the storm. It was battling to hold its roots in the ground to survive, yet I noticed how elegant it looked, despite struggling to stand its ground. I gently held its stem to capture a picture.

I thought about it that day, how resilient it was during the toughest of storms, yet so graceful. I likened it to how strong women are during the toughest of times. How resilient, yet graceful, we can be. Often, we don't notice or give women the acknowledgement they deserve, they just go about their way every day. Although struggles for them are real, their strength, dignity and grace is always upheld. So the beautiful iris inspired this poem for all women because if you care to notice, women grace us with their presence everywhere.

She is the Flower

Everything stormed around her,
The wind echoed through her,
Droplets formed like tears from her.
Yet she held strong,
Grounded by the earth beneath her,
Hopeful for the sun above her.
She found resilience within her,
She swayed gracefully in the wind,
She shared an essence of life.
Through the storm she survived,
In the rhythm of the wind,
Drenched in life's story.
She is the flower.
If you care to notice,
she is around you,
And yet she is also within you.
Be like the flower.

LOVE LETTER TO SELF

PATRICIA AHERN

For a long time, I carried a deep hidden sadness and emptiness within me. Eventually, I discovered what was the root cause; I didn't love myself. I read a quote I love; *the problem is everyone is looking for unconditional love, carrying a bag full of conditions,* I felt that. I believed I had to earn love, I had to behave in a certain way to be loved, I didn't just deserve love without conditions, and certainly not my own. Through the power of coaching, I realised some deep-seated limiting self-beliefs like; "I'm not good enough, I'm not worthy enough".

I think when we grow up in an environment of a negative reinforcement loop of judgement, criticism, blame and fear, it can feed these types of beliefs within. From my coaching journey, sadly, I am only too aware that I'm not alone and that these limiting beliefs are rife within our societies which I believe can really get in the way of us reaching our full potential.

I have spoken to people who don't treat themselves very well, but tell me that they do love themselves, they look in the mirror and are happy with what they see. However, this "love letter to self" is not about aesthetic love for self. It's not about ego love of self, it's about a feeling of worthiness, uniqueness, from within our true essence, loving ourselves more from the inside out, not only the outside in. Loving yourself whatever you look like in the mirror at any one given moment. If we shame ourselves into changing, we are in fact still stuck in the negative reinforcement, instead we can love ourselves with deep empathy into growing and evolving from a space of positive reinforcement.

I believe the journey within, to accepting oneself fully can enhance the process of finding a fulfilled purposeful meaningful life. Unconditional love, understanding and awareness of self, has helped me with my personal transformational change, and it has enhanced my life experience, and I hope it inspires and encourages others to start, or continue their journey to self-love, the purest, greatest and most fulfilling love of all. If the greatest gift you can give another is unconditional love and acceptance, remember to give this gift to yourself first and it will be even more authentic when you gift it on to another.

Many people, in response to this poem, have been inspired to write a love letter to self, I hope you will be too.

Love Letter to Self

At this time, as I do alone myself find,
I decide to write a letter from a truly loving mind.
I write, my dear, you truly are, the loving kind,
you are beyond doubt worth loving, this letter will be signed.
Oh yes you are amazing and your love you do deserve
from these loving thoughtful words, please don't ever swerve
from the unique beauty that is inside you - yes
you are as exquisite as those flowers in that bouquet,
from these thoughts please, dare not, to ever stray,
Instead, be led to the marriage of your soul, heart and mind,

so that your true love you can always find.
Don't let that love for yourself be ever shaken,
let it be that ever-fixed mark, which knows no tempest
from which to be ever shaken, as true love is never shaken.
Not by wind gale force tornado or hurricane
please do not ever love yourself in vain.
Do not to your heart admit self-defeating impediments,
Do not let your love be stained with sediments,
of unworthy, underserving thoughts, as they simply are not true,
for you are always worthy of love, for simply <u>being</u>, the miracle of you.
For when one learns to love themselves
there begins a love affair that surpasses time and space
for they shall grow old beautifully nourished full of grace
We really must be our own, before another's
so beware if in your mind, your love for you, it smothers.
Learn to love yourself and then give purely wholeheartedly
Learn to love yourself to show others how it's done gently light-heartedly
Acquire this self-love and a new world for you will have begun.
I say, this loving relationship, can be conquered, can be won.
Now place your ear upon your heart, listen, hear, it beats for you,
lay your hand on your heart, feel, how it beats for you too,
How blessed you are to have the honour of a beating heart that sings for you
Learn to love that music within and dance to the rhythm of that beat
Don't be time's fool, love yourself before it's too late
I do admit this act proves one great magnificent feat.
If it be that some or all of my letter is not met approved,
just know on the love for myself now, I shall not be moved.
So, I write this letter to myself as a gentle loving reminder
that my beating loving heart, for me, beats now much ever kinder.

THE SACRED VESSEL OF THE DIVINE FEMININE

AKLEEMA ALI

'The Sacred Vessel of the Divine Feminine' embodies the fact that the Divine Feminine is everywhere. There is no part of the Universe that does not have an element of the Divine Feminine. To acknowledge the Divine Feminine is to recognise that this sacred vessel holds the beginning of creation, the end of creation and the universe's fractal nature. The Divine Feminine should be never feared, but instead, loved and embraced; as she only multiplies into the Universe what she has been given. The Sacred Vessel of the Divine Feminine calls all women to honour their physical body, their unique life journey, their ancestors and the inner power that they naturally possess. It also encourages all women to create a new humanity, question old beliefs and shatter stereotypes; so that all women that follow and will be encouraged to be their authentic selves.

Poetry is the perfect microphone and mouthpiece that gives any individual a way to express their inner thoughts and feelings about issues that are passionate to them. There are no rules to poetry, as the words from each poet, symbolises their inner voice. Poetry merges with their personality to present to the world a soul that gets a chance to share their divine light. It is through poetry that all ages and generations bond with understanding and compassion for each other, and it is through poetry that a space is created where no topic is taboo. Poetry is unique, as it builds a person's inner confidence and self-worth so that their perspective, views and opinions are valued, allowing them to make an impact in the world with their words and voice.

The Sacred Vessel of the Divine Feminine

The vessel of divine feminine is sacred
A space and portal to enter and behold
The void of self-discovery
A physical body wrapped in layers of gold
With a lifetime between birth and death,
There are only magical stories to be told.

What mystery is awaiting you in this life
For your eyes and senses to capture
To become everything you have ever dreamed of
With no boundaries as to what and where you will create
Recognising yourself as a Goddess in human form
Yet always a playful, free spirited child of God.

To awaken the divine feminine, is to follow the beat of your own drum
Dance to your beat and follow the stream of your heart's true passion
Golden chords, twisting from Source to your present existence
Leaving footprints in the now, your eternal mark in time
Journey to the depths of your own awakening
And tell your own story before your death.

The divine feminine calls out to the lone wolf within her
To journey alone, to lead, to grow and to inspire those who observe
Those who wish to grow, to break barriers, shatter stereotypes
Those who wish to break ancestral patterns, yet honour the old stories
To tell stories of lone journeys, isolation, heartbreak and desolation

AWAKEN THE DIVINE FEMININE

And to survive and be left with only patience, love, kindness and compassion.

The divine feminine calls out to the dancer within her
To spin with the atoms of the universe
So that her identity can merge with that of Source
To blend with the resonance of Mother Earth
So that all time-lines can merge as One
To serve with divine purpose and presence
So that humanity could prosper and thrive.

The divine feminine calls out to the warrior within
Gathering all the elements, to prepare for the unexpected
To be like water, soft and flowing
To be like earth, nourishing and grounding
To be like air, purifying and reviving
To be like fire, destroy and rebuild
To be like metal, strong and purposeful

The divine feminine calls out to the Universe
To stay true to this reincarnation
And remember who we are, to be true to our inner light
To not repeat those patterns that no longer serve us
To be able to own our mistakes, flaws and transgressions
And alchemise the strings that lead to our heart.

To know that we are meant to create and manifest
A world of endless possibilities and beginnings
Where worlds collide and generational patterns dissipate
When we honour our ancestors and remain true to our DNA
Connecting all to one, and ultimately one to nothing
One truth, one harmony, one love.

The divine feminine is water, soft and flowing
Slowly creasing the earth and marking all where she has crossed
Leaving nothing untouched from her presence
Originating from the heavens from nothingness
Embracing all stages of flow from murkiness to crystal clear
Sweeping the earth until she finds her final resting point

The divine feminine is earth, nourishing and grounding
Raw, genuine, unapologetic and nurturing
She creates a stabilising and unifying field
A safe and secure sanctuary
Free to be the lioness if she wants or peaceful as a dove
Open to all who needs to rest, recharge and reflect

The divine feminine is air, purifying and reviving
Unseen yet flows through all of creation
Allowing room to breathe along her life's journey
Because her essence is not meant to be stifled
Not meant for tiny spaces, not meant to conform, not meant for stereotypes
A renewed energy and faith she brings to everything

The divine feminine is fire, destroy and rebuild
The stark contrast of total destruction
Yet, the ability to transform and build anew
To cleanse, to clear, to eradicate, to make room
For yourself, your family, your community, your planet
And the majestic stories to be written will be done so from the ashes

The divine feminine is metal, strong and purposeful
She supports, upholds, without knowing her breaking point
Yet very aware as to what corrodes her, what bends her

AWAKEN THE DIVINE FEMININE

Making her exposed and vulnerable
What matters to her is not her definition of strength
But always to where and who needs her strength.

The divine feminine is sacred,
Where whimsical fantasies meet hard core realities
Manifesting unpredictable paths, serving the collective consciousness
She is the ether, the akash, the void, the recollection
The spark that begins and will end all existence
Embrace the sacred vessel of the divine feminine.

RUMINATION ON THE GLASS CEILING

ESTER MONTGOMERY

I like to think of myself as full of potential,
Untapped fuel ready to burn.
Yet high above there's that ceiling existential,
A barrier beyond which I cannot well discern.

I have so far remained no more than a smoulder,
With a trickle of smoke rising above.
To pool against the glass that gives a cold shoulder,
And further obscure the transparency of.

I could remain here in my familiar station,
Not worrying about any challenges grand.
Tailor my actions to my own situation,
Only worrying about the problems at hand.

But I would always wonder, "Could I do better?",
Is there a way I could break through my bonds?
Is my potential just a dead letter,
Or something that to this task corresponds?

AWAKEN THE DIVINE FEMININE

There's no way to know what exactly will happen,
But I have a few possibilities in mind.
That can come as result to this tradition transgression,
Of the role by which I have felt so defined.

I can be a pessimist and so my thoughts turn,
To the very real chance of my failing.
I could try to burn hotter and yet only learn,
I was always destined for no more than flailing.

My fire within might produce only smoke,
Which does little more than make the glass above warm.
My eyes start to water and I start to choke,
And I in my grief will give in and conform.

But that is not certain and I may burn much hotter,
Driving myself to a flame incandescent.
Honing my focus and taking my chance for,
A future in which I am more than quiescent.

It would be hard but not immeasurably so,
To melt the glass ceiling that looms over me,
And as prize and punishment both have my foe,
Rain molten glass droplets in spite as my fee.

Then I would be up there unshackled and free,
Far from the life I had previously known.
I could be seen by and also go see,
A future I had only dreamed I'd be shown.

They'd see my burns and my scars and my pain,
And perhaps think that I had no more to give.
For after all I'd spent so much fuel to gain,

A position that they'd done nothing but live.

Yet I'd also have my conviction and vision,
That all I can see I can now overcome.
I have a history of breaking tradition,
The future ahead will be under my thumb.

AWAKEN THE DIVINE FEMININE

WHEN THE HARP MET THE WOODWIND

JL KEEZ

Music is a joy that delivers peace to all who hear it. Mothers have the same ability to enhance a child's life with peace. So, where music and mothers unite, harmony and joy are surely the experience for all within this reach.

When the Harp Met the Woodwind

When the harp met the woodwind
The music was exquisite

But when together they met the violin
What magic this did bring

Then along came the piano
Adding dimension to the sound

The triangle knew it could contribute
So, in unified step it tagged along

Not to miss out on all the fun
The trombone gave depth

And along with the depth
The flute added detail

With all this frivolity in the air
The harpsichord chimed in

The drum could not but help
To add its timely beat

Standing proud and ever so wanting
The clarinet tuned itself and blended in

And as if right on time
The guitar strung a chord

The symbol, well it knew
The time had arrived

To introduce the orchestra
To the guest they had formed to meet

The soloist, the one for whom they played
A guest like no other

One who carried compassion, who nurtured
Who flowed effortlessly through life

Who sang as she danced
Who caressed those for whom she cared

This was the mother of all creation
The one they all would learn

AWAKEN THE DIVINE FEMININE

Would unite the instrumental pieces together
In harmony … in joy!

PRUDENCE CLARK

When you initially fall in love with someone, it's all sunlight, blue skies and warmth right? I think we've all experienced that dopamine hit of love at some stage of our life, and this was my way of expressing it.

C.H

An untouched sunbeam
Forever radiating
Light, warmth, humour
Himself
Always…unique
         Zest like a lemon

Yet, sweet as a strawberry
Still unpicked.
A mellow beauty
Oozing from within
A light breeze
Bringing pleasure
and relief
From the scorch of the ordinary.

PERSONAL POWER

PATRICIA AHERN

My Poem, Personal Power was inspired by the book Super Brain by Deepak Chopra and R E Tanzi, reading this book was when my passion evolved for learning more about neuroscience and the brain. I realised we had negative feedback loops in the brain, the power of neuroplasticity and that we all have super brains, and we all have personal power within us. Most profoundly, it was when I first began to fully respect and appreciate the power of my own brain. Growing up there so much emphasis put on intellectual/academic intelligence (IQ), and the "brainy" people were so fortunate and would "make it big", and because I was not "brainy" or so I believed somewhere along the way, that meant, that I wasn't good enough or I was stupid or useless even, which was the thinking process that created my limiting belief.

But during my coaching journey I realised that the brain is much greater than this and our life was much more than this IQ, with other intelligences involved in our human experience like; emotional, positive, social, spiritual intelligence. This book changed everything for me, especially my conditioned thinking, the brain is always eavesdropping on the mind, change the mind and you change the brain. This book is now my "brain bible", and this poem was inspired after reading the chapter called Personal Power.

I now believe we are all born with a unique brain design and each with its own unique super-powers. There are a lot of emotionally charged self-sabotaging behaviours that get in the way of our brain power, and one included in this poem is, "self-victimisation".

In positive intelligence we call this the "victim saboteur" and saboteurs can cause us to act out self-sabotaging behaviours from negative emotions created around old survival programmes, which can keep us stuck in a negative feedback loop, the victim saboteur can tell us we are fundamentally flawed and therefore we feel powerless. But it helps to remember that a negative attitude will never create a positive life and healing happens when we take responsibility for the role we play in our own suffering. If and when we are willing to choose to release the negative power of the victim saboteur (or any self-sabotaging behaviour) and build on and listen to our intuition, our sage within, we can find our own personal empowerment which helps us to move forward in life, growing, learning, thriving towards reaching our full potential.

As Socrates said, the secret of change is to focus all of your energy, not on fighting the old, but on building the new.

Personal Power

When is the time?
When is the hour?
When will we stand up
find our personal power?
Take our life's value and worth
in our own hands
in our hearts and in our minds
making empowering stands.

AWAKEN THE DIVINE FEMININE

Being aware of self-victimisation
which can lead to lack of self-worth
and our own mental wellbeing deterioration.
So, in the long term
When will be your time?
When will be your hour?
to stand up, to find and
own that, Power?
I say;
Let this be the time, let this be the hour
Rise up and step into your own personal power.

JACQUELINE CHERIE WRIGHT

I was made to feel embarrassed, degraded and incompetent in an unwarranted display of public humiliation in a work environment, by a male colleague. Throughout the situation, I held back my tears and the more I tried to contribute to the conversation, the more aggressive he became. I walked out quietly, sat on a park bench under a tree in the park and cried. A few weeks later, I was having a coffee with an old colleague, a man I admire and respect very much. As I was explaining the situation to him, he grabbed my hand across the table and told me how respected I am by my peers and the industry, as well as how brave I am. To date, he continues to be a wonderful male leader, friend, and mentor. There are some incredibly great male leaders and friends in the world, and I am so grateful to the ones I know, as there are times when we truly need them. That man inspired this poem.

Brave

I stood there in a moment of vulnerability,
As a women in business feeling humility,
I shared my story of where I stand,
He looked at me and he held my hand.

AWAKEN THE DIVINE FEMININE

Some men stand there and tear you down,
They turn your smile into a heavy frown,
But there are men that want to hold you high,
Make you feel empowered to not deny,

That after all you've sacrificed in this life,
To be more than a mum and the role of a wife,
You've taken all the hits to have a career,
To believe that you can work without the fear

That some men impose on women in life,
As if they don't deserve to be more than a wife,
The reality is that not all men put women down,
So, surround yourself with ones that will hold your crown.

Own the moments that you have worked hard for,
Never let anyone tell you that you don't deserve more,
Trust in the ones that stand by your side,
And honour the men that fill you with pride.

I learnt in a moment that I am not weak,
In this desperate despair when I could hardly speak,
He told me I was brave and he believed in me,
The world needs more men like this to see.

Where women can show their vulnerability,
And feel equally part of humanity,
To share a story of where they stand,
And look a man in the eye to firmly shake his hand

SOUL AND SPIRIT

ANNIE GIBBINS

In a world demanding more perfection, we continue to experience the ripple effects of a woman labelled, 'not quite enough'. That is until we allow her soul and spirit to go free; unapologetic, unfiltered, unrehearsed.

Soul And Spirit

She walked with her head held high
Her spirit soaring, reaching the sky
For she knew she was more than enough
A woman, strong and tough

She had faced struggles and pain
But she had risen, time and again
For she had the fire within
To fight, to conquer, to win

She had learned to love and accept
All parts of herself, without neglect
Her flaws, her scars, her every quirk

AWAKEN THE DIVINE FEMININE

A part of her story, her own perk

She stood up for herself, and others too
For she knew the power of being true
To herself, her values, her beliefs
A force to be reckoned with, no ifs, ands, or buts

She spoke up, she took a stand
For what she believed, with her heart and her hand
For she knew the worth of her voice
A beacon of hope, of courage, of choice

She inspired others, to love and to live
To be true to themselves, to give
Their best, their all, their shining light
For they too, were enough, and could take flight

So let your spirit soar, let your heart sing
For you too, are enough, a beautiful thing
Believe in yourself, and all you can do
For the world needs you, just as you are true.

MY BUTTERFLY

JACQUELINE CHERIE WRIGHT

This was a poem I wrote to my beautiful daughter, Isabella, for her thirteenth birthday. She is gracious and elegant, need I say anymore. She goes about her ways quietly, with an air of positivity and beauty. She naturally seeks to brighten people's days, simply by passing by.

My Butterfly

She cocoons herself throughout the night,
She greets the world in the morning light.

And just like a butterfly she graces the world for all to see,
That you can make life what you want it to be.

She breathes new life into every day,
With a positive spirit, come what may.

Bringing harmony to the world from day to nigh,
Portraying the gentle nature of a butterfly!

RISING ABOVE

ANNIE GIBBINS

The noise of comparison can be deafening. The pressure of uniformity can be stifling. So, what happens when a woman rises above society's expectations? She rises from the ashes and finds freedom.

Rising Above

She used to hide, used to shrink
Used to feel like she was on the brink
Of something she couldn't handle alone
But then she found her own backbone

She realised she had her own power
Her own strength, her own tower
Built upon her every step, her every try
A fortress that wouldn't break, wouldn't die

She embraced her voice, her words
Her soul, her spirit, her birds
That soared within her heart
Telling her to play her own part

She learned to love and respect
Every part of her, every defect
For they were a part of her story
A part of her journey, her glory

She didn't need anyone's validation
She had her own path, her own station
In life, in love, in everything
For she was enough, and could sing

Her own tune, her own melody
Of life, of love, of destiny
She stood tall, she stood proud
For she knew she was enough, endowed

With all the beauty, all the strength
All the love, all the length
Of a life well-lived, well-loved
A woman, empowered, rising above.

AWAKEN THE DIVINE FEMININE

THE MIST ENVELOPES

JL KEEZ

Entwined within the female body lie elements of timeless beauty. Each time this form is created, the variation designed simply reflects how the elements combine, to produce a new rendition of the feminine.

The Mist Envelopes

The mist envelopes
Swirling in anticipation
Twisting in evolutionary twirls
Mysterious, extraordinary, serene

Held within this vision
A miracle is forming
Femininity flavouring the scene
Masculinity dispersing

For unfolding through the ether
A new, yet divine
Rendition of spirit
Filled with charm, wisdom, power

The epitome of womanhood forms

Soft, gentle, strong
For this is the creation
Birthing once more

Demonstrating the truth of the feminine
A concoction built upon timeless effort
Where in combined resolution
The female now stands

Embarking in readiness
Evolving in wonder
Bringing forth the beauty
We have come to admire

The beauty of … the feminine

AWAKEN THE DIVINE FEMININE

SHE WILL RISE

JACQUELINE CHERIE WRIGHT

This was inspired by two senior leaders I had worked alongside for a decade. We had all devoted ourselves to a wonderful business, the culture and the team were aligned and unique. With the three of us being made redundant on the same day, we took some time to re-imagine our future careers and life. It was hard to do, but I noticed a beautiful day with skies of blue and I realised, we were closing a chapter and having a new one present itself, one that would inspire hope and opportunities to each of us.

She Will Rise

From sunset to sunrise,
It may fall, but it will rise.
It creates the sparkle in her eyes,
Yesterday is a memory, tomorrow is a surprise.
And today is one of clear blue skies,
It anticipates how high she will rise.
From sunset to sunrise,
Even though it falls, it will always rise.
The sky is the limit, it is written in her eyes,
Yesterday is a memory, tomorrow is a surprise.

And today is one of clear blue skies,
Giving hope for tomorrow when she will rise.

ENCOURAGEMENT ENDURES

BRACHA GOETZ

Encouragement Endures

My father and I
Used to go to the schoolyard
Several Sunday mornings in a row.
Holding onto the back fender
Of my first two-wheeler,
He would walk,
Then run behind me,
As I rode.

I'd just keep riding along,
And then, suddenly, feeling uneasy,
I'd look back
And see my father standing there
Some distance away,
Smiling and waving.
My bike would start to wobble.
A few times I even fell.
Frightened, but determined, I went on.

And now,

Since you have Alzheimer's,
When I tell you
I'm your daughter,
And you just stare at me blankly,
I look back
And see you
Standing there,
Smiling and waving,
Still giving me the courage to go on.

WE TEACH THEM

JACQUELINE CHERIE WRIGHT

This poem I wrote to my son, Oliver. I have realised through parenting a little boy, how much of an opportunity we have to influence and teach them to grow into the best men that they can be. As women, we have a different way of understanding and nurturing boys. What a wonderful opportunity we have to teach them.

We Teach Them

Little boys are bursting with energy to burn,
They run around freely not at all worried about life's lessons to learn,
You see, it's because they believe that they can be a superhero someday,
That they can take on any situation come what may.

But their wide innocent eyes look up to us for advice as they grow,
To learn from the lessons in life that we've begun to know,
To help keep themselves out of trouble and strife,
So that they can be guided through childhood into a full abundant life.

We teach them to rise from a fall and to try once more,
That in life you can turn a tough corner and find another great thing for sure,
We inspire them to get through any challenge with an empowered vision.
To handle each hardship like it's a superhero mission.

We teach them to be a good soul and do things with pride,
We want them to enjoy the world like its one great big ride,
That no matter when they find some things hard to cop,
To rise through the lows and stand strong at the top.

With their superhero cape vision, they can take on anything,
That in any situation they can find a solution to bring,
Remembering, little boys will soon grow in to fine young men,
And they'll be armed with all the skills from when we took time to nurture them.

One day they'll be off with their superhero capes,
And we'll stand to wonder how time truly escapes,
We'll look up to them as strong, caring independent men,
And realise it was us that learned so much more from them.

I AM

ANNIE GIBBINS

No woman should shrink, lessen, or mute themselves. No woman should attempt to fit in a box too small for herself. Everyone is unique and brilliant, and declaring who we are is truly everything the world needs.

I AM

Who am I not to be me,
To hold back, to hide, to flee,
From the person I was meant to be,
And the life that was waiting for me?

I am unique, with gifts to share,
A light to shine, a love to bear,
And a purpose that's mine, and mine alone,
To live fully, and to make it known.

I won't dim my light, or shrink in fear,
Or let the doubts and naysayers steer,
For I am powerful, and I am strong,
And I know where I'm going all along.

I embrace my flaws, and all that I am,
And rise above the judgement and sham,
For I am who I am, and that's enough,
And I won't let anyone else call my bluff.

I am authentic, and I am true,
And I won't apologise for being who,
I was always meant to be, from the start,
With an open heart, and a fearless heart.

So, who am I not to be me,
To hold back, to hide, to flee,
From the greatness that I'm meant to achieve,
And the life that's waiting for me to believe.

SUNRISE

PRUDENCE CLARK

I don't fall in love easily, but when I do, I fall hard and often feel the need to voice my feelings of overwhelm and happiness, via the pen.

Sunrise

A kiss from you on the shoulder,
completeness and joy, like the
first rays of a sunrise.

Your touch, golden
irreplaceable, can almost taste it.
Your smile,
more precious than any kingdom.

Eyes like mirrors
Revealing everything and nothing
A soul so full of spirit,
It lingers on my heart like a
rolling mist on a cool morning

SHE'S THE AIR I BREATHE

JACQUELINE CHERIE WRIGHT

I was away in Thailand to take some time out, and yet was still distracted with work. My daughter sat on a swing chair taking in the beauty that surrounded her. I was in awe of her gentle nature, her beauty, and her appreciation of life - of being in the moment. It made me stop to realise how important it is that we take time to be with the people that we breathe for.

She's the Air I Breathe

She's like the air I breathe,
Through my heart she beats,
She's the oxygen to my soul,
Her voice drifts through the wind,
My ears catch her smile,
She's the joy to my spirit,
In these moments we share,
My eyes capture her beauty,
She's the essence of my dreams,
She's the air I breathe.

WHEN THAT WISP OF WIND

JL KEEZ

Have you ever felt the presence of 'someone' when in times of despair you call out for guidance? That 'someone' may well be your mother - for intertwined since birth, the strength of connection continues even in absence. Mothers are the unwavering, unconditional love that shows no bounds.

When That Wisp Of Wind

When that wisp of wind
Blows over your soul
Beckoning, encouraging

Uplifting you from despair
Caressing your brow
Drying your tears

Know that even in absence
A mother feels the suffering
Understands the pain held within

For this is the power of motherhood
The extraordinary

The bond between parent and child

This is the eternal wisp
Transcending sensibility
Overriding distance

To nurture, nourish
Give hope, engulf
In radiant acceptance

This is the reflection, innateness
Embedded within the female
Surpassing all bounds

Although momentarily felt as a wisp
Unwavering strength imparts
Empowering you, the child

To grasp this expression of care
To inhale its magnificent glow
To find comfort in its presence

For motherhood is a gift
A powerful wondrous entity
Afforded to and only found

Entwined in the one we call

… Mother

HAPPINESS

JACQUELINE CHERIE WRIGHT

I was travelling with work internationally when I met up with an old colleague and friend. We got into a conversation about life. So many of us are in search of happiness. Life takes us on a journey, and we are all learning as we go. I realised happiness isn't a destination or a 'thing'. It is an emotion that we find within ourselves. If we take time to be gracious about life, we will find it in the little things. It is within us.

Happiness

Life just takes you on a journey,
There's possibilities everywhere you can see,
But happiness is what lies deep within you,
You can find it in moments of each day that's new.
True happiness comes from inside your mind,
Even though when we visualise outcomes, we're all a bit blind,
Because what we experience can be so much more than we foresaw,
That's what makes life a journey, there's unknowns to explore.
Happiness is something to find each day,
Sometimes in the little moments that pass by your way,
But mostly you create it with the thoughts of your mind,
Remember it's your life, so to yourself, be kind.

Search for it not until your final day,
Find it in life throughout your way,
Or you'll end up wondering if it can ever be found,
When all along, your memories created it to be around
Life just takes you on a journey,
There's possibilities everywhere you can see,
But happiness is what lies deep within you,
Find it in little moments of each day that's new.

WANT

PRUDENCE CLARK

Sometimes when vulnerability strikes, all you want to do is avoid the questions, the answers and I guess, the world. This was one of those moments.

Want

I want
But you can't have.
Not in your wildest dreams
Or nightmares
Cover me.

JACQUELINE CHERIE WRIGHT

Another poem about my daughter as she stepped out in a magnificent dress for her school formal. She stood glistening in the sunlight in a bold red dress colouring the universe with her smile, warming energy and innocent beauty.

Like Sunshine

Like the sunshine bursting colour into our world,
You light up my beating heart,
Radiating with pride, adoration and love,
My eyes wide open to soak in your beauty,
The warmth emanates through my very being,
A feeling I can barely contain,
My heart filled with warmth,
Far greater than the radiating sun,
You are the colour in my world,
Through every beat of my heart.

AWAKEN THE DIVINE FEMININE

IF I CAN SAY THAT I'M FALLING IN LOVE WITH YOU

ALLY HENSLEY

There is nothing more painful than unrequited love. Whether lost love is through abandonment, grief, bereavement, or even a straying eye, falling in love with a black hole of absence can be brutal. This poem is about one woman's declaration to a man she loved, only for him to marry someone else the next day.

If I Can Say That I'm Falling In Love With You

If I can say that I'm falling in love with you,
If I can say that I'm so tired, I'm breaking
If I can whisper please, please fix this,
I can hope that we are dreams making.
If I can ask you how your wedding plans are turning real,
If I can muster up the bravery to ask your colour of quill,
If I can step away and see her joy, and angst for the big day
I can see that these moments of pleasure are cruel, and futile, let's pray.
If for me to crumble before you
If for me to say The End,
If for me to say that I let you go,

Then go, just go, don't pretend.
If I watched you for a second more,
If I retracted all that I said,
If I deleted your number like you did me,
I would have begged and begged and begged.

AWAKENING THE GODDESS WITHIN

ANNIE GIBBINS

A poem created for the tempted soul who wants more from life. When we unveil our masks to vulnerability, our flames burn brightly. Our souls light up the sky and take to the stage; unedited, unfiltered, unmuted.

Unveiling the Inner Flame

Embarking on a sacred quest within my soul,
An empowering odyssey of self-discovery unfolds,
I delve deep, in search of untold truths to behold,
Unveiling treasures hidden, stories yet untold.

Through the labyrinthine corridors of my mind's abode,
I embrace the shadows, finding solace in their code,
With each step forward, my power I reclaim,
A radiant flower, the goddess within aflame.

Shedding layers of doubt and fear, like a serpent's skin,
Embracing my authenticity, my true essence from within,
I stand tall, unabashedly and wholly me,
Diving into the depths of my divine decree.

From conformity's grasp, smouldering embers break free,
Revealing the beauty behind the ceremonial mask I see,
Empowered and fierce, I claim my rightful throne,
Awakening the goddess within, my essence fully known.

Within the depths of my being, a passionate fire burns,
Triumphantly, resilience brightly returns,
Exploring the core where my soul truly resides,
Unveiling hidden treasures, where my truth abides.

Through the maze of thoughts, I skilfully navigate,
Embracing the shadows, shaping my destined fate,
With each stride, my strength boldly reclaimed,
No longer tamed, a goddess awakened, unchained.

I shed the doubts and fears, once binding me tight,
Embracing my truth, radiating with brilliant light,
I stand tall, unapologetically and authentically free,
Embracing my divinity, proudly choosing to be me.

From conformity's cold embrace, I rise with grace,
Revealing the beauty behind the mask's trace,
Empowered and fierce, I claim my sovereign throne,
A goddess awakened, fully known and wholly grown

LET ME BE FREE

JACQUELINE CHERIE WRIGHT

As Covid kept so many of us captured in our surrounding neighbourhoods, the feeling of being let free and soaking in life's beauty and adventures again, inspired this poem.

Let Me Be Free

Let me run freely and let life begin,
Let the sea spray cold on my sun-drenched skin,
Let me dance in the sunshine with emotion to bare,
Let the wind take control and be the ruler of my hair.
I'm ready to fly, to dance from within,
Listen in silence to hear the sea birds sing,
Swallow the heaviness weighing in on my soul,
And let me breathe in life as it finds my new role.
Won't you let me run freely in this chapter to begin,
Let my spirit be empowered from within,
Ask the sun and the moon to lift the weight that I bear,
Just let the wind whisper through my tangled ocean hair.

PRUDENCE CLARK

Whenever I've experienced those early phases of love, I've always tried to write about it. I'm not sure why and it's usually for my eyes only, but upon reflection, capturing those moments takes me back to a special time in my life. Sure, love is lost, but every time I have fallen in love, I've always learned something new and gained wisdom from every relationship.

Heartbeat

Eternal warmth spreads
Enveloping all feeling, limbs
emotions of the body

Happiness spreads like an infection
Paralysing all sense and
leaving one feeling
so helpless, yet overjoyed

Radiant glow, half moon lips
bright eyes
beauty exploding from within

AWAKEN THE DIVINE FEMININE

Heart beating thrums of
pure golden ecstasy for
the other.

FLYING PAST HEAVEN

JACQUELINE CHERIE WRIGHT

Just as it says, I boarded a flight and had a memory flashback to my childhood. At that moment, I thought of my brother, Justin, who tragically lost his life at just nineteen years old. I sat quietly on the plane with the sun warming my face through the window, and as I typed this poem it flowed without thought, straight from my heart. Oh how I wished I was flying past the gates of heaven that day. My tears dropped gently off my cheeks into my lap as I slumped my shoulders and let out a deep breath. It was a moment of grace, of healing and I felt him right there with me. He has inspired so many of my poems and I write every year to help heal and share (I miss you more than you will ever know Justin).

Flying Past Heaven

When I was a little girl, I used to look up to the sky,
Just to catch a glimpse of those planes flying by.
I thought that you took a plane to visit heaven,
That made sense in my mind at the young sweet age of seven.
So, I often wondered when I could catch a flight,
To visit my loved ones to hug them tight!

AWAKEN THE DIVINE FEMININE

As the years went by I realised it wasn't true.
You couldn't just stop by heaven on a journey passing through!
Today for some reason that memory came back to me,
When I boarded a flight home I wished it could be,
That I could stop by the gates of heaven today,
To knock on the door and just say G'day,
So as I took flight on one of the many flights that I've caught,
I just had a moment so deep in thought,
I peered out my window to the beautiful sunshine and sky,
I was on one of those planes just flying on by,
I imagined just like I did when I was seven,
That I passed right by you and blew a kiss through the gates of heaven,
Just at that moment the sun beamed through the window and on to my face,
Like the warmth of a hug in that moment of grace.

ANNIE GIBBINS

To know your worth is knowing your true self. As a society, we place so much value on outcomes, but do we ever really know our own worth? Do we claim our achievements loudly? Do we apologise too often when we've nothing to apologise for? A woman's worth is hers to own, always.

A Woman's Worth

Who am I to stay small,
To ignore my dreams, and not heed the call,
To live a life that's not my own,
To stay uncomfortable and breathtakingly alone.

I am more than my doubts and fears,
More than the sum of my past years,
I have a purpose, a destiny to fulfil,
A path to follow, a dream to instil.

I am capable of greatness and more,
Of breaking through barriers and soaring soar,

AWAKEN THE DIVINE FEMININE

Of living a life that's authentic and true,
Of becoming the person I was born to pursue.

So, I will not hold back, I will not stay still,
I'll trust my heart, and follow my will,
I'll embrace my gifts, my passions, my strengths,
I'll rise above and go to great lengths.

For I am the captain of my own fate,
I am the master of my own state,
I am the creator of my own story,
I am the hero of my own glory.

So let me rise, and let me shine,
Let me embrace my life, and make it mine,
For I am who I choose to be,
And that, my friend, is the power of being me.

JUST ONE MORE MOMENT

JACQUELINE CHERIE WRIGHT

Another one for Justin, my brother, who lost his life tragically. I was searching for a sign of him on his birthday and was disappointed nothing stood out. That evening, I went out with a good friend to celebrate her birthday. I paused to ask for a seat and this young man introduced himself to me. His name was Justin and right at that moment the song I used to play on repeat as a teen played like it was on cue. My eyes just couldn't hold back the tears. I felt it was my sign, whether you believe it or not. This poem was inspired by that event and for just one moment, I imagined us there together.

Just One More Moment

Somebody told me there's a party going on,
But I've looked around and I can't hear our favourite song.
Send me the directions so I can find my way,
I'll just pop in for a moment, I promise not to stay.

To see your smile again is all I really need,
To know that you're ok, and then I will concede.
The directions to find you are nowhere to be found,

AWAKEN THE DIVINE FEMININE

Won't you play the music louder so that I can hear the sound?

Somebody told me there's a party going on,
I close my eyes and can hear our favourite song.
But there's no directions to Heaven so I can't find my way,
If only I could pop in to know that you're ok.

To see your smile again is all I really need,
I close my eyes to find it, because I need to concede.
No directions to get there but I feel you all around,
I've put on our favourite song and turned the music up loud.

I hope somebody tells you there's a party going on!
Can you hear the music? It's our favourite song…
I'll send you the directions so you can find your way,
And today for just one moment, I wish that you could stay.

JL KEEZ

Held within a tiny seed lies a new expression of feminine magnificence; each seed a beauty!

From the seed of conception

From the seed of conception
The feminine is born
A seed bound in cellular beauty
Where the links of humanity
Reflect an exquisite expression
Of caring, wisdom, thoughtfulness
A time held rendition
Magnificent in its representation

ALONE BUT NOT LONELY

PATRICIA AHERN

In a world where so much emphasis is put on being in a couple, getting married, having children and people questioning anyone who does not follow this norm, I had a belief ingrained in me that this was what normal was, and if you couldn't or didn't find that special someone to be in a couple with, there was something wrong with you, and for many years I thought there was something wrong with me, a belief I was flawed so no one could love me unconditionally.

I now understand that my deep fear of rejection played a big part in this, and my need for acceptance meant I behaved from an internal pleaser mode programme, trying to be someone I wasn't to please others. It was tiring and I now know it's an act one cannot sustain over a long period of time, as it can lead to being taken for granted which in turn leads to resentment which in itself is debilitating emotionally.

I questioned myself constantly; wondering why I was not capable of love, but now I know I didn't know how to love myself unconditionally, back then, I didn't have the emotional intelligence (EQ) or enough self-awareness of patterns of behaviour that were actually making me unhappy.

I had an idealistic view of love, not a realistic view, but fundamentally I expected someone to love me so I wouldn't feel alone, but I wasn't putting any awareness or emphasis into the process of loving and valuing myself. In relationships, I met a lot of emotionally unaware and unavailable people and then I behaved from my pleaser, rescuer, fixer mode programme, but what I learnt in the end was that it was me who needed healing from my own debilitating self-sabotaging behaviours. When I began my personal journey of growth and development, that was when I found self-love and emotional awareness building positive intelligence and since then I never feel alone. I learnt how to love me and my own company and from that place, my life of true happiness began. I love this quote from Maxwell Maltz; If you make friends with yourself, you'll never be alone.

Alone But Not Lonely

I wonder sometimes
Was I really meant to be alone
To heartbreak being prone
So long searching for the proverbial "love of my life"
"Mr Perfect", "Mr Right", so called "the one"
But only into solitude to be continually thrown
A singleton, left on the shelf,
alone, all by my little own self
What did the universe have in store
Leaving me solo, at times sad to the very core
All that time I spent, feeling damaged, so alone
Stuck, in those thoughts, in limbo,
landing and going nowhere,
just like a thrown stone
Then, myself I woke up – with an ah ha moment ,
Could I learn to love myself?

AWAKEN THE DIVINE FEMININE

Love my own company?
Find the true happiness within me?
And now, I think, from that thoughtful moment,
how I've grown
I am only **one**
but I am **one**
A solid one
A stable one
That for me, in gold
is worth a ton
actually priceless.
I have learnt to love me
in awe and wondrously
I now believe yes, maybe I was meant to be alone
But I was never meant to be lonely
I have reaped only from the seeds, for me my mind has sown
At times, I buried myself by my belief of, being damaged, being flawed,
But this was only my perceived lacking, lack of unconditional love
Therefore, my perceived unloveableness
as conventional true love, to me was somehow unknown
But how from that burial, parts of me I never knew existed,
fruitfully were grown
How could I have believed that my miraculous being was flawed
Oh, but not now, as now it's me and me alone I applaud
When we get to know ourselves
Love ourselves, belong to ourselves
nothing can ever bury us into such darkness, from which we won't rise
strong
Like the smallest of seeds into the darkness of ground, being thrown
that develop roots of which produce the sweetest fruitful results
I know now that I will leave this world alone
but never lonely

JACQUELINE CHERIE WRIGHT

I walked through the city of Sydney in awe of its beauty. As a local resident, it is not often I stop to take in the beauty I am surrounded by. One evening I stood at the base of the Sydney Opera House and these words captured my emotion, as if Sydney were a woman. She truly lights up our world.

She Is Sydney

Even in the dark times she'll help you see,
That your world is filled with all kinds of beauty.
She'll glisten as you watch her reflection dance,
You'll feel her deep sense of life's romance.
She is like no other that you could know,
Because here is her home, she's the star of the show.
But you can't take her with you when you leave,
It's in the beat of your heart that she will breathe.
Because she holds an essence of life on her own,
But she'll make you realise that you're never alone.
She is here in this lifetime,
To show that even in the dark, you can let light shine.

AWAKEN THE DIVINE FEMININE

May your eyes glisten and feel the romance,
Just live in the moment like it's your last dance.
And in the dark times be reminded of her beauty,
Because she lights up the world for you to see truly.
She is Sydney.

THE WILD WOMAN BELIEVES

ANNIE GIBBINS

A wild woman is like a temptress, a siren in the depths of mystery and power. A wild woman is poetic and her institution fierce. A wild woman doesn't need the votes of others. A wild woman owns her magic. We are all wild women.

The Wild Woman Believes

Belief is the fire that burns within,
The spark that ignites the soul to begin,
To chase the dreams that seem so far,
And trust in oneself to reach for the stars.

It's the courage to stand up and fight,
For what you believe in with all your might,
To face the challenges, both big and small,
And push through the doubts that try to stall.

Belief is the voice that whispers in your ear,
Encouraging you to conquer your fear,
To take a leap of faith and soar,

AWAKEN THE DIVINE FEMININE

And see all that you are truly capable of and more.

It's the unwavering trust in your own worth,
And the recognition of your own inherent birth,
To greatness, to joy, to a life that's true,
To the power of the belief that resides in you.

So let your belief be the guiding light,
That leads you to your heart's delight,
And emboldens you to take a stand,
To embrace the journey and seize command.

For with belief as your constant guide,
You'll find the strength to reach new heights,
And overcome any obstacle in your way,
To live life fully and seize each day.

SHE IS NEW ZEALAND

JACQUELINE CHERIE WRIGHT

I travelled to New Zealand for work and was captivated by the natural beauty, the cuisine, the people, the adventures offered. Everything about this magical place – I dedicated this poem to depict its purity.

She Is New Zealand

She radiates her energy in the daylight,
Yet she sparkles stars to light the dark night,
She mirrors her beauty from the sky to the lake,
She offers you life's adventures for you to partake,
She lets you fall in love with her authenticity & charm,
She is there to protect and to do no harm,
She tantalises your tastes with the flavours of nature,
She warms your soul with her dancing spirit and culture
She colours your world as she kisses the sun away,
She shines a smile when the moon lights the way,
She reveals the stars just for you to see,
That magic happens when you let life be
You'll take with you her memory forever to keep,
Because she grounds you, yet gives you so much to reap,

AWAKEN THE DIVINE FEMININE

She encapsulates the beauty of life where you stand,
She is tranquil, yet adventurous, she is pure New Zealand

JL KEEZ

If we were asked to describe 'the female' using colour as its description, I wonder if this would be the result?

The Cauldron of Life Beckoned

The cauldron of life beckoned
The warmth its calling card
The swirling pattern encased
The beauty to behold

Held within its care
A colourful mixture blends
Weaving its threads together
To form a time held vision of greatness

The blue haze of kindness
The red of fiery strength
The purple of transformation
The white of purity

AWAKEN THE DIVINE FEMININE

As the colours merge
A sprinkling of feminine power
Dusted from above
Adds a golden lustre

The yellow of spring chimes
The green of new beginnings sprout
The turquoise of abundance grows
The magenta of wisdom wove its magic

Then from this cauldron of grace
Of creative awareness
A spiral transcended
With all the colours integrating

The picture of exceptional radiance
The combination of solidarity
The heralding of innocence
The formation of uniqueness

Stood divinely in our presence
For this cauldron had yet again
Given birth to the one we know as female
The embodiment of empowered love

The personification
The manifestation
The incarnation
The intrinsic

A truly mind-blowing work of art …

EXPERT ON TRUE LOVE

BRACHA GOETZ

At 8:30 in the morning,
Into the clinic he'd come.
Stitches needed to be removed
From the old man's thumb.

But he kept glancing at his watch.
What was he waiting for?
The young doctor just asked him,
Before he walked out the door.

"What is it you are rushing to?
Where do you have to be?"
"I have breakfast with my wife," he said.
He said it eagerly.

"Every single morning,
Soon as the clock strikes nine,
I am there to eat with her.
That is how we dine."

AWAKEN THE DIVINE FEMININE

"My wife is in a nursing home.
Her dementia has progressed."
"So would she care if you were late?"
The intern asked, in jest.

"She doesn't know who I am.
She hasn't known in years.
But I still know who she is."
He said, smiling through tears.

JL Keez

The power, the expression of the female, manifests from a seed planted and nurtured so in empowered understanding the role assigned may not only live in wisdom, but also share the knowledge of what being female is; allowing those assigned to stand strong within the eternal feminine existence against change that time does bring.

From The Seed of Life

From the seed of life
Manifests a glorious being
Weaving its magic
An embodiment of spiritual excellence
Dancing in the moonlight
Clasping hands in prayer
Swaying to an unheard beat
Bowing in empowered acceptance
That the being incarnating
Is timely in creation
For this is yet another
Feminine in nature

AWAKEN THE DIVINE FEMININE

Designed to spread its wings
To enlighten those within its path
For this is the role assigned this human expression
To entangle those within its reach
To learn the art of being female
So generations to come
Will forge ahead in strength
Understanding that forebears held the knowledge
As to what being female meant
Ensuring the magnificence
Continues, evolves, stands firm
Against the changing tides of time ...

SHE IS THE SPIRIT OF ALOHA

JACQUELINE CHERIE WRIGHT

Immersed in Hawaii while on holiday, I took a breath and in total awe and appreciation, I understood the spirit of Aloha. These words came to me like a beautiful Hawaiian song drifting through the salty haze of the ocean breeze. Hawaii is a place where you want to soak in the beauty, the culture, the locals and you always leave feeling more enriched.

She Is the Spirit of Aloha

She started the day with a breath of fresh air,
She breathed life into her soul,
She filled her spirit with a sense of beauty,
She shined with radiance to start the new day,
She offers tranquillity, her warmth is intense,
She has depth, yet she makes way for you in the shallow,
She starts your day with a breath of fresh air,
She breathes life into your soul,
She fills your spirit with a sense of beauty,
She makes your smile radiate from the inside,
She is the balance between tranquillity and intensity,
She has depth, but she makes way for you in the shallow,
She is the spirit of Aloha.

BLUSH

ALLY HENSLEY

A meaningful deep dive into a non-negotiable type of love. This poem untangles a version of love that one woman depicts as perfect. We all strive for belonging, connection, affection, and desire and by understanding the role of love, we can find it. For those who are falling in love, or recovering from heartache, this poem acts as a soul contract. Only when we know what we do and don't want from love, can we surrender to the search and wait for 'this type of love' to find us.

Blush

It's the kind of love that makes your hands clammy and your eyelids flicker
The kind of warmth that makes sleeping easy and waking sweet
It's the smell of corks popping and ovens roasting
It's the kind of magic that tickles hearts and nose-tips when dreaming
It's the noise of phone calls, when the waiting becomes sickening and scary
It's the handprint on a sofa-cushion as he leans in for the first kiss
The colours soar like summer and autumn burning; it's that kind of love.

It's the kind of love where eyes speak within moments of silence,
The kind of chill that breaks humidity and sweat
It's the surface that feels like years and years of woven silk
It's the kind of cosmic journey when meditation perfects itself
It's the golden cup of coffee with a layer of frothed milk as the papers arrive
It's the white shirt creased against his biceps that makes the female eye squint in awe
The labyrinth of stories and teenage tunes unravel; it's that kind of love.

It's the kind of love that makes the ocean sound louder
The kind of swirl you wish to be caught under
It's the feeling of salt drying through you hair; tousled, blonde and free
The kind of peace and lead like snoozing, as the sun laces the nape of your neck
It's the smell of summer; of crushed berries and honey juice, lotion and sandy grains
The feeling when day meets the night, and you're soon to be with him
Where shadows walk you home; it's that kind of love.

It's the kind of love that encourages fear and self-loathing,
The kind which offers you a way out before your heart should break
It's the worry and wanders; if you deserve and if you're pretty enough
It's those mornings where you awake to find no message, no mail
It's one of those evenings where songs no longer play, and the air feels cluttered again
It's the feeling where your heart is on leave, and there's no news of its return
The pain is very real, and the days seem twice as long; it's that kind of love.

AWAKEN THE DIVINE FEMININE

It's the kind of love where he knocks on your window, where words fall freely and slow
The kind which hands you back hope and harnesses your falling
It's the kind which smiles and assures
It's the kind that whisks you off without warning or need for clothes
To places where clothes are voided and cheap
It's the kind of weekend where time has no meaning or place in your humble nest
It's moments like this where your life leaves the room; it's that kind of love.

It's the kind of love that melts enemies and creates heroes
The kind that offers hope like a 1920's film
It's the voice as you put your key in the door and the butterfly peck greets your cheek
It's safe and curvaceous; it's steeped in pure beauty,
The kind that makes you dizzy and walk taller, walk prouder
The sad days are less sad, the happy become the best
Where you never stop fearing its potential loss, where you always pinch yourself for its presence,
It's that kind of love.

SHE IS DUBAI

JACQUELINE CHERIE WRIGHT

I had the incredible opportunity to travel to Dubai for a conference, and given I am in the travel industry, I was captivated by how much this destination has to offer - the experiences, entertainment, elegance and majestic class. On the other hand, the natural surrounds of the desert dance its way from day to the glistening lights of the city at night. No matter what, Dubai glistens from morning to night and that inspired this poem.

She Is Dubai

She soars high like she can reach the sky,
She glistens before the sun falls to nigh,
She awakens with the beauty of night,
She brings a smile to the city of light.
She opens her eyes to see a new day,
She stops for no one in her way,
She burns in the heat of her own pace,
She does not falter, she stands strong with grace.
She is as intricate as each grain of sand,
She is as complex as the centre of a desert land,

AWAKEN THE DIVINE FEMININE

She is the essence of life to those who know her,
She is to others just a fleeting moment of adventure.
She awakens with the beauty of night,
She smiles gracefully through the city of light,
She soars high to reach the sky,
She glistens through her spirit, after all, she is Dubai.

THE SOUNDS OF EXPRESSION

JL KEEZ

In a world where females are often quietened, a few stand against the words of condemnation. In doing so, the unadulterated truth of the feminine demonstrates an expression of empowerment where the joy of internal freedom allows authenticity to reign.

The Sounds of Expression

The sounds of expression
Emanating through the door
Brought forth a curiosity
Wistful, evoking, playful

Closer examination was required
Stepping closer with care
The door appeared to understand
That knowing was the objective

Slightly beckoning
The hinges turned to the left
A sight of purity greeted
Dancing, spirited, divine

AWAKEN THE DIVINE FEMININE

And this my friend
Is the unadulterated
The truth of the feminine
Long before life interfered

You see
Life has a way of bulldozing
Robbing us of authenticity
Demanding quiet from those who dare

Yet for those who choose to question
Empowerment grows strong
Delivering the greatest of gifts
The return of the natural

A force of nature confident
To be the woman designed at birth
To be the woman our world deserves
For this is the woman

Explicit in her truth
Ignoring the voices of others
Rising from the ashes
To ordain, impart, consolidate

Why being a woman is
A reconcilable power
Where underestimating her worth
Is an unquestionable exercise!

THE BEAUTY BENEATH

ANNIE GIBBINS

We need less mirrors and touch-up apps. Deep down, beneath the skin, the bones, the blood, dances unwavering strength and beauty. No lipstick, no heels, no blow-dries. This is the beauty beneath.

The Beauty Beneath

In a world obsessed with perfection
Our bodies bear the brunt of rejection
We're bombarded with images of the ideal
As if our worth is defined by how we appeal

Our curves, our shape, our size, our skin
All scrutinised, criticised, judged within
We're told to conform to a certain mold
To hide our flaws, to fit the prescribed code

But what if we looked in the mirror and saw
The beauty within, the strength that we draw
From every curve, every mark, every scar
A reflection of who we are

AWAKEN THE DIVINE FEMININE

Our bodies are more than just vessels
They are home to our souls, our treasures
They carry us through every step of the way
Through pain, through joy, through every day

So, let's celebrate our bodies, big or small
For they're a testament to our journey, our all
Let's love ourselves, just as we are
For we're beautiful, just the way we are.

WHO WILL I CALL

JACQUELINE CHERIE WRIGHT

Dedicated to my beautiful mum, Helen, to acknowledge and thank her for lighting up my life like the sun. I was having the toughest of times and I called my mum, my confidante, my best friend. I wept my way through my rambling words as she comforted me and made me see through to the light twinkling in the distance that everything would be okay again. I just can't imagine life without her and when I wrote this, I was so incredibly grateful that I am still blessed with being able to pick up the phone and call her. Yet I still wonder who I will call when I can no longer call mum?

Who Will I Call

Who will I call if I can't call my mum?
Who will be there to warm my heart like the sun?
Some days I'm living life to my heart's desire,
Other days I'm lost and it can feel so dire.

But who will I call if I can't call my mum?
Who will be there to warm my heart like the sun?
When I try to find comfort there's only one person I call,

AWAKEN THE DIVINE FEMININE

No matter what happens she's there through it all.

So who will I call if I can't call my mum?
Who will be there to warm my heart like the sun?
Sometimes the little things are not big at all,
But there are some days I still trip and fall.

And it's you that I pick up the phone to say hey mum..
Your voice warms my heart like the fire of the sun.
I wish we had a million years to come!
And I know one day I won't be able to call on you mum…

And then who will cheer me on even though I haven't won?
Who will take my calls when I need to turn to someone?
I'm so grateful for the years we've had here together.
And as we both get older, It's inevitable that our time won't last forever.

So I am holding on to the comfort in your words that I hear,
For this special time that I still have you near,
Because who will I call when I can't call my mum?
To replace you, there will never be anyone.

THE LOVE POEM

ANNIE GIBBINS

Not every poem needs to be dedicated to a 'love' opposite us. Some loves deserve to be handed to ourselves; the permission to stop, listen and be. Not every love poem needs a perfect ending to an inner perfectionist. Some love poems are meant for those who wrote them.

The Love Poem

Goodbye to perfectionist me,
Who always strived for what couldn't be,
Who never felt quite good enough,
And always felt like a piece of fluff.

Goodbye to the constant pressure,
To always be better, to always measure,
Up to impossible standards and goals,
That only served to take their tolls.

Goodbye to the endless striving,
That left me feeling so unfulfilling,
Chasing a dream that was never real,
A never-ending cycle that I couldn't heal.

AWAKEN THE DIVINE FEMININE

For I am ready to embrace,
A new way of living, a new pace,
One where I am enough as I am,
With no need to be perfect, no need to cram.

I'll learn to embrace my flaws,
And accept myself, without any pause,
I'll give myself grace, and take it slow,
And let go of the need to always grow.

So goodbye to perfectionist me,
And hello to the person I'm meant to be,
One who's flawed and beautiful and true,
A person who's worthy, just like you.

JACQUELINE CHERIE WRIGHT

Dedicated to my Dad, Harry (Habib). Having spent many years apart in different countries, Covid reunited us for a few years. I am so grateful to have had some time back again. It made me realise how much he had aged, but yet how strong he remained. I love his words and his laughter, his spirit of life. Through the toughest of times and distance we always have remained so close. I am so incredibly grateful and wanted to gift him and to honour him with this poem for Father's Day, just as he turned 80.

Dad

The first name was yours that I learnt to speak.
Soon I could call, 'let's play hide and seek!'
The first hands were yours that I held to walk,
Soon I could say, let's sit down, have a talk.
The first steps you watched until I could hold my stance,
Soon I could say 'come along, let's have a dance'.
Now the phone rings your name for us to speak,
We chat about life and all that we seek.
You now hold my hand as we go for a walk,

AWAKEN THE DIVINE FEMININE

I listen intently to hear you talk.
We both stand steady as we hold our stance,
And still you light up the room when we have a dance.
Time is passing quickly and I cherish we can still speak,
I hold on to your words to live what I seek.
Your hand still guides my path when I stumble to walk,
And I hold onto the words to get me through as we talk.
You steady me to take an empowered stance,
Until I hear the music, to embrace life's dance.
One day you'll be gone and we will not speak,
So now it is simply just time with you that I seek.
To hold your hand gently as you walk,
And remember the words that you endlessly talk.
I'm inspired by the strength of your stance,
Please, let's find a moment soon to have another dance.

JL KEEZ

Where trauma lines the life events of childhood, dreams will come forth to inform the child, now a woman, as to why her body hurts. Through exploring the contents, messages will inform. Through examining the messages for truth, healing will emerge.

Laying Nightly Upon Her Pillow

Laying nightly upon her pillow
Unrest joined her dreams
Flashes of indiscretion invaded

Morning found brief respite
Her days filled with fear
Interrogation lingered
Answers did not form

With tiredness overtaking
Again the pillow called
Dreams of discontentment ensued

AWAKEN THE DIVINE FEMININE

The brief respite of morning
Diminished over time
The dread of nightly visions
Disturbed her daily world

In time awakened terror
Drew tears of despondent calls
Her pillow, thrown to the floor

With sleep loudly summoning
And a body drained of strength
Slumped against the mattress
Tiredness won

Peace enveloped her mind
Dreams danced in joy
Waking delivered energy

The respite so often carried
Now replaced by smiles of wonder
Her body once folded in pain
A vessel of magnificence

In puzzled thought as to how
She grasped the discarded pillow
Immediately acknowledging the weight

This pillow, her nightly refuge
Had been her companion in life
This pillow had heard her story
Cried throughout the years

Her pillow she understood

Carried the pains born from her past
Had grown heavy with the burdens bestowed

In caring desperation this pillow
Had given rise to the nightly terrors
Delivering memories in attempt
To awaken and set the woman free

As understanding joined her
She set the pillow free
Through shredding she disposed the pains

Tears, grief, anger
Accompanied the action of dismantling
And as the last piece was torn
She sighed in noted acceptance

Her pillow wished to remind her
Of the events from life that tormented
Requiring her attention

The confining of her soul
Tortured from traumas past
Were held within her pillow
Awaiting the day when in readiness

The inherent characteristic
Attributed to this female
Would emerge triumph

Drawing from deep within
The toughness, the capacity

AWAKEN THE DIVINE FEMININE

To endure the agony
Of life's healing hand

For this is the greatest of traits
Existing, cocooned, woven
Within the female body

The ability to rise against the odds
To manifest remarkable, outstanding
Incredible power
To overcome, to reclaim, to transform

From adversity, through adversity
The one once born pure
To again reflect the purity

The pillow always knew
Was there …

JACQUELINE CHERIE WRIGHT

I wrote this about new love, Paul. There is something so special about when we meet someone and hear of their dreams and aspirations, and how they envision their future chapters to be. To be captivated by someone, so that you feel a small part of their journey with anticipation, before the chapters evolve makes you realise you have become part of the story.

His Story

His eyes share a story as deep as the sea,
They go far beyond what I could imagine could be,
Coloured with reflection of the sky so blue,
I listened as he told me a story or two.

Diving the ocean and how amazing it is,
Hiking through mountains in these adventures of his,
Now, about to set sail on a new journey ahead,
I listened to his dreams while on his chest lay my head.

I could see a little sadness of moments in his eyes,
Through the closing of chapters in each new sunrise,

AWAKEN THE DIVINE FEMININE

But there is a spirit of adventure and dreams to come,
And with each day the light & warmth of the sun.

I know that the days will come and go,
But through each one I hope he will know,
That the world may be big but it is also small,
And to find a solution, I know who to call.

Our eyes now share a story as deep as the sea,
They go far beyond what I imagined could be,
Coloured with reflection of the sky so blue,
I became a small part in this story so true.

PRUDENCE CLARK

A glass of wine, a storm outside, the flickering lamp. If that's not ingredients for a love poem, I'm not sure what is.

Passion, or Merely Summer?

You radiate humidity
pressure before a storm
Electrifying, suffocating, inescapable.

I can taste your presence,
swallow your smell
absorb your sweaty ocean salt…
Unquenchable thirst

Parched.
Will love you
till the seas run dry.
Drain me.

LIFE PLAYS A TUNE

JACQUELINE CHERIE WRIGHT

This poem is in honour of the relationship I had with Dave, a man I was deeply in love with and devoted to for over two decades, he was my husband and is the father of my children. This is the story of the courage and strength that we kept drawing from each other, to keep the rhythm of our union, our partnership and our love. Even during the most testing times. This was a time when we still had hope of making it rhyme, before we would eventually lose our way.

Life Plays a Tune

Life is a journey, it doesn't really take long,
There are times you walk to the beat of a song,
And there's times when it doesn't even rhyme,
It's just taking the next step, one step at a time!
Life is a journey, we're not walking for long,
There are times when you need to stop to stand strong,
There are times when it doesn't even rhyme,
And it's just taking the next step, one at a time!
Life is a journey, the last tune played has gone,
But there's that time when you wait for the next song,
That time is the time when the music will rhyme,
And it's just taking the next step, one step at a time!

Because life is a journey, it really doesn't take long,
The time has come to dance to the next song,
The music is playing a new tune this time,
And we're dancing together in what's meant to rhyme.

MAKE YOUR MARK

PATRICIA AHERN

Not long after I wrote my poem Personal Power, I wrote this poem "Make your Mark", as I now believe when you choose to take that personal growth journey within, to understanding your uniqueness, your personal power, building self-love, you are on your way to reaching your potential.

Victor Frankl said, *the meaning of life is to give life meaning*, I believe when we find our meaning in life, we make our mark. I use poetry to support and encourage proven coaching tools, for example writing a personal mission statement, which has been described as *'creating our own self-identity, a global narrative about oneself, coming from within, like a moral compass, in which we are capable and adaptable'*. We also can master our integrity of self with daily positive self-affirmations which protect us against self-doubt and negativity which can hinder our performance and growth towards our potential.

Personal mission statements became part of university entrance application as it is realised that *"having a personal mission statement brings clarity and positivity and can ground us and give us a sense of inner stability to have at times when we need it most"*. When we put feelings into words it's like pressing the pause button on our emotional responses and our autopilot reactions, it then gives us time to reflect on our written words with more clarity.

I write from the heart to tell my story of transformational change, including messages of hope and positivity and possibility. The subtle art of coaching has helped me to do this and I do believe we can inspire, not by perfections but by our imperfections, our human vulnerabilities, our unique life experience and story. Never underestimate the positive power of a person who has found their meaning in life and who shares unconditional compassion and empathy, honesty, kindness in the world, and how that ripple effect can spread far and wide. In a world with far too much hate, create your positive personal mission statement, make your mark and move mountains of negativity. Remember what you feed grows negativity breeds negativity and positivity breeds positivity, choose what you feed on your journey to making your mark.

Make Your Mark

Make your mark be free
too many people I know
are way too unhappy
as they age never feeling
they've made their mark
as their inner selves they've kept in the dark
so go for it now, create your story
Go with your own personal glory
know that it will come from within
so light up, step up and begin.
Create your own reality,
your own solemn plea
Write your own personal mission statement.
Your story from which there'll be no abatement.

AWAKEN THE DIVINE FEMININE

to what you can do, to what you can achieve
write it, take action and believe
don't keep that power of you in the dark
step into your power and make your mark.

JACQUELINE CHERIE WRIGHT

I wrote this poem for the man who was my husband for two decades, Dave. On our 22nd wedding anniversary, I shared these words as it became public that we had moved on to go our separate ways forward. I wish him love and light, always and forever.

Guided Light

You've been my guiding light,
From darkness into light.
You've been the one to care,
Always been there.

You've been there through it all,
Watched me rise and caught my fall.
You've loved my heart through every beat,
When I won and then felt defeat.

You've pushed me to succeed,
Working for what we need.
You've held my hand,
Through every demand.

AWAKEN THE DIVINE FEMININE

You've cradled my heart,
Even when we were apart.
You've held my dreams,
Through tears of streams.

You've believed in me more than I would,
Shown me I'm more than I thought I could.
You've carried me through,
With a vision brand new.

And I've stood there with you through it all,
Watched you rise and caught your fall.
I've loved your heart through every beat,
When you won and then felt defeat.

I've pushed you to succeed,
Working for what we need.
I've held your hand,
Through every demand.

I've cradled your heart,
Even when we were apart.
I've held your dreams,
Through tears of streams.

I've believed in you more that you would,
Shown you more than you thought you could.
I've carried you through,
Now here we stand with a vision brand new.

I hope you know I've been your guiding light too.
From darkness into a light that's new,

Always know in your heart how much I care.
Near or far, I'll always be there.

SILENCE OF HER SMILE

JACQUELINE CHERIE WRIGHT

Written for my little sister, Julie, as I witnessed her journey over the years from the first moment, I shared with her that we had tragically lost our brother, Justin. Her big brother. She was just 17 years old. I silently watched on through her darkest moments in the depth of despair, to the beautiful beaming light she has now found in her heart. She has a sense that he is always with her, in her memories, in her dreams. It carries her through. It carries us all through. He is forever walking to the beat of her heart. He is the protector of his little sister.

Silence Of Her Smile

Her smile silent, nowhere to be seen.
Her breath caught in the moment, what did it mean?
Words suffocated her heart, unimaginable to repair,
Her small frame crumpled as she fell in despair.

Her smile silent, with a glimpse to be seen,
Moments of memories, knowing what had been.
In time she let go of the relentless fight,
Her mind soon could seek the light.

Her smile silent, with a glimmer to be seen,

Moments gone past and the ones in between.
She carried on through, finding strength and hope,
She let her heart breathe, found a way to cope.

Her smile silent, it shines to be seen,
He is there when she closes her eyes to dream.
She feels him walk to the beat of her heart,
As she graces this world, she knows they are never apart.

I AM A DREAM CHASER

ANNIE GIBBINS

To awaken our divine feminine, we must reach for the absolute stars. We must learn to think big, think brighter, and think about all the dreams we've ever imagined. We, me, us – are all dream chasers. Together, let's turn our dreams into the most exquisite realities a woman could ever imagine. .

I Am A Dream Chaser

I am a dream chaser, with passion and drive,
A fire burning within, that keeps me alive,
I set my sights high, and I aim for the stars,
And let nothing stand in the way of my heart.

I am a believer in the power of dreams,
The magic they hold, and the hope they bring,
I chase them with fervour, with courage and might,
And keep pushing forward, into the light.

I face my fears head-on, with grit and grace,
And keep moving forward, at my own pace,
For I know that every step is a part of the climb,

And with each one, I'm closer to making them mine.

I surround myself with those who believe,
And lift me up when I need to achieve,
For in this journey, it's not just me,
But a tribe of dreamers, who help me see.

That anything is possible, if we just believe,
In ourselves, in our dreams, and all that we achieve,
For we are the dream chasers, the makers of change,
And with each step forward, we'll make a world of a better place.

So, let's chase our dreams, with all that we've got,
And believe in ourselves, even when it gets tough,
For we are the dream chasers, with the power to thrive,
And make our wildest dreams come alive.

SHE IS LOVE

JACQUELINE CHERIE WRIGHT

This poem was written about searching for love. In a moment where I was in search of love, I took a picture of a beautiful rainbow in tropical north Queensland over the ocean. It inspired this poem, in that a woman's love has all the grace and beauty of nature, finding its place in the world and showcasing all she has to offer. With a heart in search of deep love, she puts her vulnerable self out there, as pure and beautiful as nature can be. Waiting to be found.

She Is Love

She sails like a mystery from one ocean to the next
She tip toes onto the shorelines and dances through the wilderness
She travels through the wind like the scent of jasmine
She's has the untouchable beauty of a rainbow
She spans from here to there
She seeks to comfort you through the storm
She sings through the birds at dawn
She radiates like warmth through the sun
She glimmers and shimmers like a silhouette in the starlight

She is drenched in life's promises
She finds truth in the breaking dawn
She pulls the tides like the moon
She knows you search for her
She is here.
She is there.
She is everywhere
She is love
Waiting to be found

WELCOME TO ME

PATRICIA AHERN

I have used writing for myself for years not aware of the phenomenal research behind writing and its benefits in terms of self-expression and therapeutic value. Due to the loud voice of my inner critic within, I would not have believed that any of my poetic stories were interesting or good enough to share. However, during my coaching journey, as my inner world changed more positively empowered, so too did my thoughts, feelings, beliefs, and then my desire to share my writings has grown stronger. However, sharing life stories of innermost feelings and thoughts can be quite daunting as in doing so we also share our vulnerabilities, hidden secrets, fears, pain, and that can be quite scary.

This poem "Welcome to Me" speaks into the fact that each one of us is on our own unique journey in life, and no two journeys are the same. As Maya Angelou said, "we are the sum total of everything we've ever seen, heard, eaten, smelled, been told, forgot – it's all there". Our human existence is full of experiences good to exhilaration and bad to suffering and everything in between. I think we are conditioned to just want the good all the time, but when we realise the bad times, the challenges and losses really do help make the good times even better, and they can heighten our sense of appreciation and gratitude in life for the good things and even the little things. All our challenging difficult life experiences can help us to persevere, and they can help us build resilience within, each can be a wonderful teacher. When we become aware of this process it helps us to believe we can get through the bad times and the losses, seeing it through to the good times, and the beautiful times again. Every single experience we have in life, is the sum of our life existence, and we can learn something from each experience. I love this quote from Ziad K.Abdelnour, "to be the best you must be able to handle the worst". Self-belief is a superpower we can all find within us and I'm glad I found my path from low self-esteem to self-belief and empowerment, which is forever a beautiful work in progress. For self-expression creative writing is amazing but I now share because I care, with a desire to inspire, to take you on a journey to the divine beauty that resides within you, albeit dormant sometimes, please make a vow to yourself that you will no longer hide it within you, but instead let it shine.

Welcome to Me

Welcome to me
and all you cannot see
As so much I did hide
All those tears I cried
Welcome to me
On the outside, is only
ever what your eyes did see
not who I wished I was
or could ever be.
Welcome to me
the dark, the light
the love, the fight
the ache, the pain

AWAKEN THE DIVINE FEMININE

the strength, the gain
the highs, the lows
the kisses, the blows
Welcome to me
to the times I felt less
that emotional mess
I lived, I died, I cried
I laughed, I smiled, I tried
to keep the fear
from showing,
for compassion and love
to keep growing
Welcome to me
all those parts, to see
right from the heart
of me,
and all the things
you cannot see
until I let you in
to who I am and
where I have been
to my life story now
I've opened that door
If you want to know more
I'm ready, explore
my poetic stories
So welcome to me
I hope you like
what your eyes could never see

FEIRCE AND FEMININE

ANNIE GIBBINS

Is there any other way to be? I know deep within us all, sits a unique and magnetic power. And we shall call this power, 'fierce and feminine'.

Fierce and Feminine

In the depths of my being, I uncover boundless grace,
A tapestry of femininity, woven with love's embrace,
With each heartbeat, I celebrate my inner might,
Blooming like a flower, radiant with my inner light.

Through the gentle sway of my hips, a dance unfurls,
Expressing emotions, as my soul's story unfurls,
I embody softness, resilience, and unwavering power,
A warrior goddess, fierce and beautiful, hour by hour.

With every tender touch, I mend and heal,
Embracing the power to nurture, love, and feel,

AWAKEN THE DIVINE FEMININE

From the depths of my core, strength surges through,
A wellspring of courage, eternal and true.

In the whispers of intuition, my guiding star,
Trusting the wisdom that resonates from afar,
I embrace the divine rhythm of my soul's melody,
A symphony of femininity, bold and free.

In the sacred union of vulnerability and grace,
I navigate life's labyrinth, finding my rightful place,
Embracing femininity, a masterpiece of sacred art,
Revealing the goddess within, heart to heart.

ABOUT THE POETS

Annie Gibbins is a true Renaissance woman, with accomplishments in every facet of the business world. As an acclaimed TV and podcast host, keynote speaker, #1 best-selling author, publisher, and business mentor, Annie has established herself as a leading voice for women in business. Despite her numerous accomplishments, Annie's story is one of resilience and determination. She has successfully raised a family of five, including two sets of twins born only 26 months apart, all while building an incredible 7-figure business empire. Through Women's Biz Global, Annie has mentored countless women from around the world, helping them to achieve their goals and reach their full potential by calling out limiting beliefs, clarifying purpose, and developing strong business practices. Annie's story is a shining example of the incredible heights that can be achieved with hard work, dedication, and the right mindset. Her journey inspires women everywhere to break down barriers and achieve their wildest dreams.

Australian author and poet, Jacqueline Cherie Wright, affectionately known as Jac Wright, captures the emotion and essence of life's moments in a collection of heartfelt, inspiring work through her own divine feminine experience of life's lessons, love, and loss. Born and raised in Sydney, to immigrant entrepreneurial parents, her father being Egyptian and mother Anglo-Indian, she had a diverse upbringing in the 1970's and 80's. It was when she was nine years old that she first discovered her love of poetry in a school competition, however, not until her adult years did she start sharing her poetry on love, loss, little ones and lifestyle, with family and friends. With a celebrated career in tourism and a mother of two to Isabella and Oliver, she finds time in her quiet moments to write. She is humbled when her words resonate and have meaning to others.

Five years ago, Patricia found herself miserable, lost, burnt-out and stuck in a negative reinforcement loop. That is when Patricia found coaching and with self-awareness, she began to recognise that her life was running on outdated beliefs and thought patterns that were no longer serving her, yet she still relied on them, unaware that they were so emotionally draining and debilitating. Through the power of coaching and building on this self-awareness, she believed more and more in the possibility for her to create a better life for herself, and a path to true happiness. Patricia believed this could happen if she gained autonomy, learning to take ownership of her life and her emotions and so her journey of writing her own life story began. Now, Patricia loves and values the power of her creativity like never before. She loves writing for self-expression, creating poetic stories to inspire and share messages of hope and positivity. Most of all, Patricia loves creating stories with the message, 'you are not alone', in this life experience. Fundamentally, Patricia has learnt that self-awareness is where the journey of personal growth begins, it is the key to transformational change, as Anthony de Mello said, "what you are aware of, you are in control of; what you are not aware of, is in control of you". Self-awareness enables us to recognise our options, those options give us personal choices, in turn, those choices give us agency and agency develops our personal power and an inner peace and freedom, which for Patricia is always a work in progress, and is a beautifully rewarding process. A process that Patricia wishes for you too. Reach out to Patricia at hello@pacoaching.co.uk.

Akleema Ali is the proud owner of The Reiki Lighthouse in Trinidad and Tobago. She creates a sacred space and sanctuary for those wanting to get more grounded in life, take charge of their emotional healing, gain clarity and welcome more peace and calm in their lives. Akleema has several publications on the theme of mental health and wellness including her journey with Reiki, her story of completing a 1000-day gratitude practice, gateways to happiness and the practice of meditation. She promotes and highlights Reiki as a method for relaxation, peace and calm that can be used by all individuals, regardless of ethnicity, religion, social status and abilities. Akleema is also a motivational speaker and loves to participate in humanitarian projects. She uses the language of poetry as a healing instrument, as well as an art form to convey her unconditional love and oneness with humanity.

Survivor of a nine-year struggle with anorexia nervosa, and many more enduring associated debilitating, mental illnesses, including chronic fatigue, migraines, anxiety, OCD, depersonalisation and suicidal depression, JL Keez dedicates her life to empowering those impacted as she once was. A Reality Therapy Certified Counsellor, Speaker and Teacher, J.L. Keez's detailed insights are powerfully portrayed in her first memoir, 'Anorexia Unlocked: Understanding Your Story Through Mine'. JL's second book, 'Recovery, and All That Jazz: Mental Illnesses, Life Events and True Understanding', dives deep into the development of mental illnesses, recovery and empowering life moving forward. She particularly highlights the role of relationships. JL's third book, 'Echoes From My Heart; my words gifted to you to comfort, guide, inspire' is a collection of verses. Her passionate delivery for The Reality Therapy Institute, Australia, on the topic, "How We Relate ... Impacts" demonstrated her strength as an inspirational voice within her subject area. Speaking for Rotary International, where mental health concerns were discussed, exemplified her gift for presenting. J.L. Keez educates sufferers of mental illness, with a focus on eating disorders, through educational programs, zoom webinars, inspirational speaking and books.

AWAKEN THE DIVINE FEMININE

Prudence Clark has always had a flair and passion for writing and after studying a degree in Journalism and a Masters in Journalism and Creative Writing, she has never put the pen down. With astute editing, copywriting and proof-reading skills, Prudence is able to produce the words you want, when you want. With vast copywriting and editing experience over a range of industries, including tourism, health, construction, publishing, music and the arts, Prudence takes pride in developing creative and engaging copy that inspires not only clients, but also readers. Her love of words also drives her passion for poetry and she believes there is nothing more therapeutic than writing prose, with a glass of wine in hand. When she's not writing, you can find Prudence at the beach, book in hand or in the garden, swimming in the ocean with her son, or tending to her vegetables.

Ally Hensley is an author, speaker, ghost-writer, content creator and stigma shaker of the best kind. Ally produces engaging, relatable, and insightful content for some of the world's biggest brands and emerging start-ups. Ally – as a creator of several global campaigns – understands how to reach big audiences with new ideas. As a versatile writer, Ally personalises her projects with authenticity, knowing that behind any brand is a backstory, with limitless potential towards vision and sales. As a passionate storyteller, Ally is determined to make truth-telling through words, the next biggest trend. Dedicated as ever, Ally has held the position of Board Trustee with MRKH Connect since 2021, Europe's go-to charity for MRKH support and awareness charity.

Bracha Goetz is the Harvard-educated author of 42 books that help children's souls shine, and she has also written a candid memoir for adults about her journey to joy, Nourish the Soul.

www.ingramcontent.com/pod-product-compliance
Lightning Source LLC
Chambersburg PA
CBHW030119100526
44591CB00009B/458